Mental Prayer

An Easy Method

by
Rev. Bertrand Wilberforce O.P.

All booklets are published thanks to the generous support of the members of the Catholic Truth Society

CATHOLIC TRUTH SOCIETY
PUBLISHERS TO THE HOLY SEE

Contents

What is Mental Prayer? 5
  The soul speaks to God 5
  God knows our thoughts 6
  In spirit and truth 7

The Importance of Mental Prayer 8
  God won't force us 8
  Living in God's grace 10

Is Mental Prayer Easy? 12
  Difficulties often imaginary 12
  Quite easy and simple to do 13

Mental Prayer - Preparation 15
  Adoration of God present in your soul 16
  Sorrow for sins preventing union with God 16
  Ask for light 17

Mental Prayer - Body of the Prayer 18
  Meditation and study 18
  Problems to avoid 19
  Conversing with God 21
  Start at the beginning 22

Approaching God 24
  Faith 25
  Humility 25

    Confidence 25
    Thanksgiving 26
    Contrition 26
    Love 26
    Loving repentance 28

Petitions 30
    Petitions and resolutions 30
    Value of petition 31
    Ask for graces you need 33

Resolutions 35
    Faults and virtues 35
    Be practical 36

Mental Prayer - Conclusion 37

Final Encouragement 38
    Why is mental prayer so complicated? 38
    Are all these things to be done in this precise order? . . . 38
    How long should mental prayer last? 40
    When is the best time for mental prayer? 40
    I have no time for mental prayer 41
    Where should I do mental prayer? 42
    What book shall I use? 3 42
    But I become so distracted 45

Endnotes 46

What is Mental Prayer?

Prayer, says St Gregory Nazianzen, is conference or conversation with God. St John Chrysostom calls it a discoursing with the Divine Majesty; according to St Augustine it is the raising up of the soul to God. St Francis of Sales describes it as a conversation of the soul with God, by which we speak to God and He to us, by which we aspire to Him, and breathe in Him, and He in return inspires us and breathes on us.

The soul speaks to God

All prayer then is the speaking of the soul to God. This may be done in three ways; for the prayer may be either in thought only, unexpressed in any external way, or on the other hand the secret thoughts and feelings of the soul may be clothed in words; and these words again may either be confined to a set form, or they may be words of our own, unfettered by any form and expressing the emotions of our soul at the moment. In the first case our prayer will he purely mental; in the second, in which we employ a set form of words, it will be vocal prayer; in the third case, where the prayer is chiefly in thought, but these thoughts are allowed to break forth into words in any way that at the moment seem best to express the feelings of the soul, it is a mixture of mental and vocal prayer; but as the words are spontaneous and not in any prescribed form, it may justly be considered as mental prayer.

God knows our thoughts

In an audience with the Pope, we might read a written address to His Holiness, or we might trust to the words that might occur at the moment to express what we desired to convey to his mind. But if God were to enable the Pope to read the thoughts of our mind, we might then simply stand silent in his presence, and he would see all that we wanted to express. The formal address would be vocal prayer, the silent standing before his throne would be purely mental prayer, the conversation with unprepared words would be a mixture of the two, and might be called mental prayer in a more general and extended sense. God knows our secret thoughts more clearly than we can express them, more certainly than we ourselves can know them; and words therefore are not necessary in our intercourse with Him, though often a considerable help to us.

A set form of words spoken or read cannot be called prayer at all unless the mind intends it as prayer, and gives some kind of spiritual attention, either to the actual sense of the words themselves or to God Himself while they are being uttered. Shakespeare spoke as a theologian when, in *Hamlet*, he put into the mouth of the King, who asked for pardon without repentance: "My words go up, my thoughts remain below; Words without thoughts never to heaven go."

In spirit and truth

God condemned the merely material homage of the Jews by declaring, "This people honour Me with their lips, but their heart is far from Me." All prayer, therefore, of whatever kind, must be "in spirit and truth: that is the kind of worshipper the Father wants." (*John 4, 23*); but vocal prayer is confined to a prescribed form of words, whereas mental prayer is the spontaneous utterance of the soul either with or without words. When St Francis said an Our Father, or recited his office, he used vocal prayer; when he knelt before God without a word, his prayer was purely mental; when he spent the whole night in saying "My God and my all," his mental prayer was mingled with words which expressed the burning love of his seraphic soul.

The Importance of Mental Prayer

Prayer of one kind or another is absolutely and indispensably necessary for salvation - in other words, no one who has come to the use of reason, so as to be capable of prayer, can, according to God's ordinary providence, be saved without it. This necessity is proved in the first place from the distinct, emphatic and constantly repeated command to pray, and to pray continually. For instance: "Then he told them a parable about the need to pray continually and never lose heart." (*Luke 18, 1*); "You should be awake, and praying not to be put to the test. The spirit is willing but the flesh is weak." (*Matt. 26, 41*); "Ask and it will be given to you; search and you will find; knock, and the door will be opened to you." (*Matt. 7, 7*); "Be persevering in your prayers and be thankful as you stay awake to pray." (*Col. 4, 2*); "Pray constantly" (*1 Thess. 5, 17*).

God won't force us

Besides these positive commands it is evidently necessary; because though God really wills the salvation of all, (*1 Tim. 2, 4*), He will not save us without our own co-operation. He will save no one by force: for heaven is not the land of slaves, into which men are driven by compulsion; it is the home of the free children of God, of those who love God, of those who are free with the freedom with which Christ has made us free.

Therefore God gives to all the grace to pray; and if they use this grace and continue to pray aright, He will continue to bestow on them a chain of graces that will end in salvation. But to those who will not pray, He has promised nothing: "He is close to all who call him, who call him from their hearts" (*Ps 144, 18*). "The nearer you go to God, the nearer he will come to you. Clean your hands, you sinners, and clear your minds you waverers." (*James 4, 8*).

From this absolute and indispensable necessity of prayer in general, we can easily infer the importance and the moral necessity of the best and highest kind of prayer - namely mental prayer. If not absolutely it is certainly morally necessary in some form or another even for salvation; and there can be no manner of doubt that it is strictly necessary for any real advance of the soul in virtue and divine love. St Alphonsus says: "He who neglects meditation (a part of mental prayer), and is distracted by the affairs of the world, will not know his spiritual wants, the dangers to which his salvation is exposed, the means he ought to take to conquer temptations; and will forget the necessity of the prayer of petition for all men: thus he will not ask for what is necessary, and by not asking God's grace, he will certainly lose his soul."

Living in God's grace

In the same way St Teresa asks: "How can charity last, unless God gives perseverance? How will the Lord give us perseverance if we neglect to ask Him for it? And how shall we ask it without mental prayer? Without mental prayer there is not the communication with God which is necessary for the preservation of virtue." The holy Doctors agree that those who persevere in mental prayer will live in God's grace. The following words are the deliberate sentence of the holy Doctor St Alphonsus, the conclusion gathered from his vast learning and experience: "Many say the Rosary, the Office of Our Lady, and other acts of devotion, but they still continue in sin. But it is impossible for him, who perseveres in mental prayer to continue in sin: he will either give up mental prayer or renounce sin. Mental prayer and sin cannot exist together. And this we see by experience; they who make mental prayer rarely fall into mortal sin; and should they have the misery of falling into sin, by persevering in mental prayer they see their misery and return to God. Let a soul, says St Teresa, be ever so negligent; if she persevere in mental prayer the Lord will bring her back to the haven of salvation."

If this were merely the opinion of St Alphonsus himself it would be of immense weight, considering his resplendent sanctity, his vast spiritual learning, and the varied experience of his long and active life; but besides this the holy Doctor is here only summing up in one sentence the teaching and experience of all the doctors, saints, writers, preachers, and confessors of the whole Church since the beginning. What stronger argument could be used to prove the importance and necessity of mental prayer?

Is Mental Prayer Easy?

Anyone who has a real desire to be saved, and who believes that the opinion of St Alphonsus and all other spiritual teachers - that mortal sin and mental prayer cannot live together, but are mutually destructive - is really true, but must feel a desire to adopt so certain a means of salvation. But many are fainthearted, and dread the little difficulty they feel in beginning a new exercise; and many more lack the courage and self-denial necessary to continue in it after the novelty has worn away, and the yoke of perseverance begins to gall. Blessed are they who courageously persevere, for their salvation is secure!

Difficulties often imaginary

Those who find it difficult to begin, or are tempted to abandon this powerful means of salvation, must pluck up heart, and encourage themselves by remembering that mental prayer requires no learning, no special power of mind, no extraordinary grace, but only a resolute will and a desire to please God. In fact, the hard matter is to convince people how easy and simple a matter mental prayer really is, and that the difficulty is far more imaginary than real. This difficulty often rises from not having grasped the true idea of what is meant by mental prayer; and the false idea of the exercise, once formed, is often never corrected, the consequence being that the practice is either abandoned in disgust, or persevered in with extreme repugnance and little fruit.

One common cause of misunderstanding, perhaps the most common of all, is the custom of calling the whole exercise by the name of one subordinate and not the most important part - that is, meditation. From this the idea arises that it is a prolonged spiritual study, drawn out at length with many divisions and much complicated process; and this notion frightens many good souls, and makes them fall back on vocal prayer alone. They imagine that the soul must preach a discourse to itself, and they feel no talent for preaching. Many, if they spoke their minds clearly, would say: "I cannot meditate, but if I might be allowed to pray during that time instead, I could do very well." This is no imaginary case, as anyone who has had any experience will testify; and this miserable misunderstanding, that so often holds souls back for years, is partly brought about by defective teaching, but partly also by the name meditation being used instead of the more comprehensive one of mental prayer.

Quite easy and simple to do

Mental prayer properly understood, will be found to be easy and within the power of all who desire salvation. Of course there are many degrees of prayer, and to pray perfectly is no doubt a matter of great difficulty; but to pray well, and in a way very pleasing to God and very profitable to the soul, is an easy and simple matter. If we remember how many thousands have excelled in mental prayer, though not even able to read, we shall see that this holy exercise cannot require any special power of mind or any degree of culture. St Isidore, a farm labourer, is an example of a man utterly devoid of human learning, but rising, by God's grace, to the sublimest prayer.

The following method of making mental prayer is drawn from the works of St Alphonsus, who may justly be called the Doctor of Prayer; and it is so simple that no one who studies it with any attention can fail to understand it, and all who reduce it to practice will find that in great measure it takes away the difficulty they may feel in the exercise. Many who have found "making a meditation" to be a wearisome penance, have experienced that with this method the time is all too short; and that conversation with God is indeed the greatest joy of life; "Taste and see how sweet the Lord is."

All methods of mental prayer are essentially the same. They are different ways of reaching the same end, the object of all being to teach the soul how she can converse lovingly with God. In the method recommended by St Alphonsus, the whole exercise is divided into three parts: - the Preparation, the Body of the Prayer, and the Conclusion.

Mental Prayer - Preparation

The real preparation for prayer is a good life, a spirit of recollection enabling a person to live in God's presence, and the invaluable habit of regular spiritual reading. But this is not the place to enter into these matters, and so we must proceed to the immediate preparation, when the time of prayer has come. "Prepare yourself before making a vow, and do not be like a man who tempts the Lord" (*Eccles. 18, 23*). From this admonition of the Holy Spirit, it is evident that we must not presume to throw ourselves down before God unprepared, our minds full of idle, distracting thoughts, and imagine that we can thus pray in a way pleasing to Him. How careful should we be to prepare both body and mind if admitted to a papal or a royal audience! At least then make in preparation for your conference with God, three short though fervent acts:

1. An act of faith in God's presence, and of adoration, profound and humble, of His majesty.

2. An act of contrition for sin, sin forming the cloud thick and dark over our heads that hides the brightness of God's face. "But your iniquities have made a gulf between you and your God. Your sins have made him veil his face so as not to hear you." (*Isaiah 59, 2*).

3. A fervent petition for light to see God's holy will, especially in some one matter either pressing upon us then or suggested by the subject we are going to consider, and for grace to do God's will when we do see it.

Examples of these acts may help beginners, but it must be clearly understood that they are only examples and that they may be made in any form.

Adoration of God present in your soul

My God, I believe that You are present with me and within me, and I adore You with all the affection of my soul. Be watchful," says St Alphonsus, "to make this act with a lively faith, for the remembrance of the presence of God is a great help to keep away distractions. Cardinal Carracciolo, Bishop of Aversa, used to say that distractions are a sign that the soul has not made a lively act of faith."

Sorrow for sins preventing union with God

O Lord, by my sins I deserve now to be in hell; I repent, O infinite Goodness, with my whole heart of having offended You. I am sorry for sin from the bottom of my heart; have mercy on me.

Ask for light

O Eternal Father, for the love of Jesus and Mary, give me light in this prayer, that I may profit by it. Then add a Hail Mary, a very short word to St. Joseph, your Guardian Angel, and your holy patrons.

These acts should be short. In a mental prayer of half-an-hour, not more than three minutes should be devoted to them. But at the same time they should be fervent and earnest, the whole attention being given to them; for upon the manner in which they are made will, in great measure, depend the fervour of the whole prayer.

Mental Prayer - Body of the Prayer

In order to pray with fruit and without distraction, it is very useful, and in most cases necessary, to spend some time in meditation, or pious thought, on some definite subject; and from this fact, as before stated, the whole exercise is often called meditation, instead of mental prayer. This often misleads people into imagining that meditation - that is, the use of the intellect in thinking on a holy subject - is the main end to be aimed at, whereas in fact it is prayer, or conversation with God.

Meditation and study

Meditation furnishes us with the matter for conversation, but it is not itself prayer at all. When thinking and reflecting, the soul speaks to itself, reasons with itself; in prayer it speaks to God. Meditation, in its wide sense, is any kind of attentive and repeated thought upon any subject and with any intention; but in the more restricted sense in which it is understood as a part of mental prayer, it is, as St Francis of Sales puts it, "an attentive thought, voluntarily repeated or entertained in the mind, to excite the will to holy and salutary reflections and resolutions. It differs in its object from mere study: we study to improve our minds and to store up information; we meditate to move the will to pray and to embrace good. We study that we may know; we meditate that we may pray".

We must then use the mind in thus thinking or pondering on a sacred subject for a few minutes; and in order to help the mind in this exercise, we must have some definite subject of thought, upon which it is well to read either a text of Holy Scripture, or a few lines out of some other holy book - St Teresa tells us that she thus helped herself with a book for seventeen years. By this short reading, the mind is rendered attentive and is set on a train of thought. Further to help the mind, you can ask yourself some such questions as the following: What does this mean? What lesson does it teach me? What have I done about this in the past? What shall I now do, and how?

Problems to avoid

Two remarks are here most important. The first is that care must be taken not to read too much, but to stop when any thought strikes the mind. If the reading is prolonged - if, for example, in a short prayer of half-an-hour you were to read for ten minutes - the exercise would be changed into spiritual reading. The second remark is, that you must not be distressed if you find the mind torpid, and if only one or two very simple thoughts present themselves. It is by no means necessary to have many thoughts, nor to indulge in deep and well-arranged reflections. The object prayer is not to preach a well-prepared and sermon to yourself - the object is to pray. If one simple thought makes you pray, why distress yourself because you have not other and more elaborate thoughts? If you wanted to reach the top of a roof, you would not trouble yourself because your ladder was a short one, provided it was long enough to land you safely on the roof. The end is gained. If one simple reflection enables you to pray, you would, in reality, be merely distracting yourself from prayer, in order to occupy yourself with your own thoughts, if you were to go on developing a lengthy train of thought. This would be to mistake the means for the end, and it is a very common mistake, and the cause of great discouragement. This mistake will be evident if you remember that while you are following out a line of thought-for instance, when you are answering the questions suggested above-you are conversing with yourself.

It is plain therefore that as your object is to converse with God, you should not remain too long in talking to yourself, and that therefore, if you feel a difficulty in doing this, you need not be distressed. "The progress of a soul," says the enlightened St Teresa, "does not consist in thinking much of God, but in loving Him ardently; and this love is gained by resolving to do a great deal for Him."

Conversing with God

I have said that misunderstanding this point is the most fruitful source of discouragement and one of the commonest reasons for abandoning mental prayer in disgust; and the reason is, because very few people are accustomed to prolonged or deep thought on any subject few indeed are capable of it. If therefore they imagine that prolonged if not deep thought, is necessary for mental prayer, they are in constant trouble and discouragement, which ends in their abandoning the whole exercise in despair. "If I might only be allowed to pray," they will sigh to themselves, "how much easier it would be!"

Let such persons then clearly understand that many thoughts are not necessary, that their reflections need not be deep and ought not, especially in a prayer of half-an-hour, to be long, lest prayer should be neglected and the exercise be changed into a study. "Meditation," says St Alphonsus," is the needle which only passes through that it may draw after it the golden thread, which is composed of affections, petitions and resolutions." The needle is only used in order to draw the thread after it. If then you were to meditate for an hour and think out a subject in all its details, but without constant acts and petitions, you would be working hard with an unthreaded needle.

Our minds differ as much as our features, and some, especially those employed in very distracting duties, need more thought than others before they can pray; but many will find that the effort, after prolonged reflections, will generally defeat itself, and end in distraction.

Start at the beginning

As soon, therefore, as you feel an impulse to pray, give way to it at once in the best way you can by acts and petitions - in other words, begin your conversation with God on the subject about which you have been thinking. Do not imagine, moreover, that it is necessary to wait for a great fire to burn up in your soul, but cherish the little spark that you have got. Above all, never give way to the mistaken notion that you must restrain yourself from prayer in order to go through all the thoughts suggested by your book, or because your prayer does not appear to have a close connection with the subject of your meditation. This would simply be to turn from God to your own thoughts, or to those of some other man.

One useful suggestion may here be introduced. Those who are accustomed to make regular spiritual reading will often meet some idea, or passage of their author, which strikes their mind forcibly, or seems especially suited for their own practise. When this is the case, they could not do better than to take that idea, or that passage, as the subject of their next mental prayer. As they have read about it and thought about it in the time of spiritual reading, a very slight reflection will be enough to enable them to pray upon that subject with solid fruit, and to make practical resolutions concerning it.

We have spoken thus far of the needle: now we must proceed to consider the golden thread which, is the matter of principal importance, and should occupy the chief part of the time devoted to prayer. The golden thread is composed of: Affections or Acts, Petitions and Resolutions - a triple cord of beauty and strength, which, when the soul uses earnestly, "she puts her back into her work and shows how strong her arms can be" (*Prov. 31, 17*).

Approaching God

Acts, or affections of the will, are the movements of the soul towards God. The affections are called the feet of the soul, because by them she approaches to or recedes from God. To "draw nigh to God" does not mean any bodily motion, but the spiritual progression of love. When therefore in meditating on a subject you feel some holy sentiment arising in your heart, begin to make simple acts, with or without words, to God. Acts of this nature are very various, such as faith, hope, confidence, humility, thanksgiving, contrition, love. They should be simple, short, and often repeated. Think of our Lord's prayer in the garden, which is intended as a model to us. He prayed for three hours, and His whole prayer consisted in the constant repetition of one single act of resignation and petition. The word "Acts" will suggest the chief aspirations that it is well constantly to repeat: A stands for Adoration; C for Contrition; T for Thanksgiving, to which is joined love; and S for Supplication, the prayer of petition.

These acts should be spontaneous, springing up from your own soul, but some examples may help beginners. If then you were to take as the subject of your prayer the death of our Lord Jesus Christ on the Cross, you would, after the preparatory acts, begin to think of the mystery.

"Who is that hanging on the Cross?", you would say to yourself: "What is He suffering, in body, in soul? Why does He suffer?"

Faith

Not many minutes' thought would be necessary before you would feel moved to acts of Faith: "O my Lord, hanging on the Cross, I believe in you. You are the Eternal God, made man for me. You are my Redeemer; for my sins You are bleeding and dying on the Cross.

Humility

"O my Jesus, I am not worthy to live. I have slain You, the Son of God. Who am I, dear Lord, that You, the everlasting God, have suffered and died for me! I am Your creature, made by Your hands. I am Your rebellious child. I deserve hell for my sins, I deserve to have been abandoned by You, and yet You have thought of me and offered Yourself as a victim for me. How good You are, dear Lord, to be nailed to the Cross for so miserable and ungrateful a sinner! I will not sin again."

Confidence

"If I look at myself, dear Lord, I am filled with fear. I have sinned, O Lord, against You, my sins are more in number than the hairs of my head. How shall I dare ever to hope for pardon, after having so often and so basely offended You! But Your death is my hope. You have made me, I am Yours, and You have suffered for me, and died for me. I hope in You, in You do I put my trust, and I shall not be confounded forever. You will not reject me now that I repent, when You have shed Your Blood for me."

Thanksgiving

"I thank You, O Lord, with all my heart for Your great goodness in dying for me, and shedding all Your Blood for me. Blessed be Your holy Name! I thank You for not abandoning me when I committed that sin, for loving me in spite of all my many sins against You. Blessed be Jesus, who shed His precious Blood for me! Most holy Mary, help me to thank Your Son for all He has done for me."

Contrition

"I am heartily sorry for all my sins. I detest them all, and especially because they have displeased You, because they have nailed You to the Cross. Lord, be merciful to me, a sinner! Father, forgive me, for I did not know what I was doing."

Love

"I love You, my Jesus, I love You, but I do not love you as I ought; make me love You more and more. I love You with my whole heart. I desire to see You loved by all. I will only what You will. You have died for love of me, I desire to die for love of You; I rejoice that You art eternally happy. Do with me and all that is mine according to Your will." "This last act of love and oblation of self," says St Alphonsus, "is especially pleasing to God, and St Teresa used thus to offer herself to God at least fifty times in the day."

Acts of love should be frequent whatever the subject of meditation may have been. "The act of love," continues the same Saint, "as also the act of contrition (which is sorrow founded on love) is the golden chain which binds the soul to God." *An act of perfect charity is sufficient for the remission of all our sins.* "Above all, never let your love for each other grow insincere, since *love covers over many* a sin." (*1 Pet. 4, 8*).

Sister Mary of the Crucified once saw, in a vision, a globe of fire, in the flames of which straws were instantly burnt up. She was thus made to understand that when the soul makes acts of love to God, all her sins are consumed in the flames of charity and are forgiven. Besides, the Angelic Doctor, St Thomas Aquinas, teaches that by every act of love, we gain a fresh degree of glory. "Every act of charity merits eternal life." How many we can make in the course of the day, if we have some little fervour, especially during the time of mental prayer!

Loving repentance

St Francis of Sales has the following consoling and most instructive words concerning acts of sorrow founded on love, or, as he styles them, acts of loving repentance. "Because this loving repentance is ordinarily practised by elevations and raisings of the heart to God, like to those of the ancient penitents: I am Yours, save me! Have mercy on me, O God, have mercy on me; for my soul trusts in You! Save me, O God, for the watershavee come in even, "unto my soul! Make me as one of Your hired servants! O God, be merciful to me a sinner! It is not without reason that some have said, that prayer justifies; for the repentant prayer or the suppliant repentance raising up the soul to God and reuniting it to His goodness, without doubt obtains pardon, in virtue of the holy love which gives it the sacred movement. And therefore we ought all to have very many such ejaculatory prayers, made in the sense of a loving repentance and of sighs which seek our reconciliation with God; so that by these laying our tribulation before our Saviour, we may pour out our souls before and within His pitiful heart, which will receive them to mercy"[1]

As already stated, these acts or affections should spring from the heart; we must not look for fine words nor make up grand sentences; the mere movement of the will towards God, with love, gratitude, hope, and sorrow for sin, is sufficient even without words. Therefore does our Lord say: "Do not speak much when you pray" - a simple movement of the heart is better than many words proceeding merely from the lips. Nor should we hurry from one affection to another. If you feel yourself moved to make acts of love, keep on making acts of love; if you are excited to sorrow, repeat acts of sorrow for a while, till the affections grow cold; then pass on to another. Moreover, these affections should be made slowly, allowing the soul to dwell upon each act. It is well to make slight pauses between. God often speaks to us during these pauses, and when He does - when we perceive some good thought in our mind giving us some new light, a clearer insight into ourselves or a better knowledge of God, or showing us our duty or God's will for us - then we should listen humbly while God speaks, prepared to obey His commands.

Petitions

Besides the acts and affections of the soul - all of which are truly prayer, since the soul, in making them, converses with God - it is extremely useful to occupy ourselves during mental prayers in making many fervent petitions to God for His spiritual graces and favour. This prayer of petition is a matter that St Alphonsus, in all his ascetical works, is continually urging upon every soul in language the most emphatic.

Petitions and resolutions

Indeed, our Lord Himself has given us the first lesson as to the necessity of constant petition, not only by His command "Ask and it shall be given unto you," but by the fact that the Our Father, the model of all prayers, consists half of affections and half of petitions for what we need. In English, we have not anyone word that expresses this kind of prayer, and we are obliged to call it prayer of petition. The French word *la prière* expresses it, while *l'oraison* means mental prayer with its acts, affections, and resolutions. This distinction explains many passages in the works of St Alphonsus for instance, where he says, "Without prayer (that is, petitions for graces) all the meditations we make, all our resolutions, all our promises will be useless. If we do not pray (that is, if we do not make petitions for graces) we shall always be unfaithful to the inspirations of God, and to the promises we make Him. Because in order actually to do good, to conquer temptations, to practise virtues, and to observe God's law, it is not enough to receive light from God, and to meditate and to make resolutions, but we require moreover the actual assistance of God, and He does not give this assistance except to those who pray, and pray with perseverance."[2]

Here is the distinction between meditation with resolutions, or mental prayer in general, and prayer of petition, or between l'oraison, and la prière.

Value of petition

Without this distinction, which is not at first apparent in English translations, much that is said of prayer is confusing and unintelligible. For instance, in the above extract the Saint appears to say that mental prayer without prayer is of no avail. Again in his "*Rule of Life for a Christian*," in that most valuable volume called "*The Christian Virtues*," the second rule is about mental prayer while the sixth is concerning prayer. Again we understand that prayer means prayer of petition, the difficulty vanishes. In his constant exhortations to the practise of prayer of petition, the holy Doctor is fond of quoting the experience of that learned and enlightened writer, F. Paul Segneri, S.J., who thus speaks of himself: "When I began and before I had studied theology, I used to employ my time of mental prayer in reflections and affections; but God opened my eyes afterwards, and from that time I endeavoured to occupy myself in petitions, and if there is any good in me I consider it to be due to this habit of recommending myself to God."

Petitions, therefore, for all you need, are a very important part of mental prayer, and are most useful to the soul. But a caution is necessary here to prevent misunderstanding. The petitions in the time of mental prayer should be spiritual petitions - that is, for spiritual objects, such as forgiveness of sin, love of God, light to see, and grace to do God's will. For if the petitions were for temporal favours, such as health of body for yourself or others, success in business, rain or fine weather and the like, two inconveniences would follow. In the first place it is always doubtful whether such things are according to the will of God or not, and they must be asked for only if they should be the Divine Will, and the whole spiritual value of the petition will then be in that act of resignation. Secondly, the mind would be much distracted from God in order to think of the matters upon which to form petitions, and especially if the subject of the petition should be some person in whose temporal welfare you are much interested, or some worldly business that gives you anxiety - to pray for these things would probably result in distraction. The mind would begin to reflect upon the things themselves and forget God.

By this it is not meant that these temporal matters must never be made the subject of prayer, but only that it is not generally advisable to occupy the mind with them during mental prayer, for the reasons given. The truth is that all these things are suggestions from experience; for in the matter of mental prayer, in which "the Spirit blows where He wills," there are very few "musts," few things of which you can say this *must* be done.

Ask for graces you need

With this understanding as to the subject matter of petitions, the soul cannot be better occupied during mental prayer than in making frequent and earnest petitions, in the name of our Lord Jesus Christ, for all the graces she feels to need. Ask, then, for help in the time of temptation, beg grace always to persevere in prayer when tempted, but particularly remember always to pray for the three following graces, which, if you obtain, will render your salvation secure. These three all-important graces are: (a) The perfect forgiveness of past sin; (b) The perfect love of God; (c) The grace of a holy death. Christ our Lord, Truth itself, has promised distinctly and emphatically, "Ask and it will be given to you; search, and you will find; knock, and the door will be opened to you" (*Matt.7.7*). "And if you have faith, everything you ask for in prayer you will receive." (*Matt.21,22*). Ask then for these three graces, which, by their very nature, must be according to God's will that you shall have; ask for them with humility, confidence and perseverance, and they must be given to you. God's promise cannot fail. Ask for the perfect forgiveness of all your sins, and, however many and grievous they may have been, forgiveness will be yours. Seek for the love of God by many earnest petitions, and you shall find it. Knock at Heaven's gate by constant petition for a holy death, and the golden gate of that city of love and peace will be opened to you, as your eyes close in death, and your soul departs into eternity. "Pray," exclaims St Alphonsus, "pray, and never give up praying. If you pray, you will certainly be saved; if you do not pray, you will certainly be lost." We have so many spiritual wants, that half-an-hour's prayer will be all too short to make our earnest petitions before the throne of mercy.

Resolutions

In order to make mental prayer truly fruitful, you should be careful to make some definite and precise resolution, either to avoid some fault or to practise some virtue. Mere thought, it is evident, cannot make us holy. Acts and affections by themselves will not make us practise virtue. Even petitions by themselves are not enough. They obtain for us, it is true, the strength to conquer sin, and to do what is good; but the most difficult matter remains that is, to use this grace, and actually to do what we recognise to be God's will.

Faults and virtues

We must, then, make a resolution to carry out into practise what we see to be good. How frequently, from want of this steadfast resolution, men pray for a grace, but in their actions deny and contradict their prayers! The resolution should be often repeated, day after day, until we can easily keep faithful to it. Moreover, it should be definite, that is, not too general and vague. A determination for instance, to be better than we have hitherto been, to he humble, to love God, is of no practical advantage whatever. It means nothing, it will begin and end itself, and produce no effect on our daily life; we must therefore resolve to avoid some particular fault into which we are likely to fall that day, or to practise some one act of virtue that very day.

Be practical

The resolution moreover must be of a practical nature - that is, it must be something that we can do if we please; and above all, it must be sincere, by which is meant that we must truly intend in our hearts to carry it into practise when the opportunity occurs. It may be perfectly sincere at the time, even if we are weak enough afterwards to fail in its practise, but there is no excuse if we are insincere at the time of making it. That would surely be insulting to God, who sees the heart. We must never forget the words of St Teresa, already quoted: "The progress of a soul does not consist in *thinking* much of God, but in *loving Him ardently*, and this love is gained by resolving to do a great deal for him." Make then *one practical, definite* resolution that you can keep and mean to keep that very day.

Mental Prayer - Conclusion

Before rising from your knees, three short but fervent acts should be made, as the finishing stroke of your mental prayer:

1. An act of thanksgiving for the lights and graces that God has given you during your prayer. For instance: "I thank You, O my God, in the name of Jesus Christ, for all the help You have given me. Blessed be Your holy name. Glory be to the Father."

2. Renew earnestly the good resolution you have already made.

3. Ask for grace to keep it. You can address this petition either to the Eternal Father, begging Him, through the merits of Jesus and the intercession of Mary, to grant you this favour; or, you can address our Lord Himself, or you can beg the prayers of our Lady or your patrons. Lastly, make a short prayer for the conversion of sinners, and for the souls in purgatory.

Final Encouragement

A few concluding remarks may be useful, in order to remove difficulties that often arise and discourage the souls who feel drawn to give themselves to the holy and delightful exercise of prayer.

Why is mental prayer so complicated?

"There seems so much to remember, so many things to do!" When the method of prayer is drawn out step by step on paper this is quite true. It does look a complicated affair, and so would everything else if it were thus minutely described. Try to set down on paper all that we must remember in order to eat and drink in a polite manner, and see how formal and complicated it all seems; but do it, and it at once appears easy and natural. It is the same with mental prayer. Practise it for a short time, and all its difficulty will vanish.

Are all these things to be done in this precise order?

The preparation will always come first, with the three short fervent acts, and the conclusion will always naturally be at the end; but in the body of the prayer no formal order is to be observed. That part should indeed always begin by a short meditation, some simple earnest thoughts, but the Acts and Petitions should come forth from the heart in any way that they arise. In describing them we must adopt some order that the matter may be intelligible; but in practise they can be all intermingled in any way in which they spring from the soul. Remember, the end and object of the whole exercise is to converse with God; if you are doing this therefore you are doing well. I have said that there should always be some short meditation, because I am speaking to beginners of whom this is true; but for those more advanced this becomes less necessary, and after a time might be only a distraction. If the mind is all day long full of worldly and distracting thoughts and imaginations suggested by business, amusements, conversations, study, light reading, and so on, it is evidently necessary to think of some holy subject in order to be able to pray with any fervour or recollection. When, on the other hand, a person leads a quiet, secluded life, with few distractions, regular spiritual reading and frequent reflection on spiritual subjects, the soul is very easily moved to pray, and less meditation is necessary. After a time, with holy and contemplative souls, any train of thought would become a distraction; they are at once, and without effort, absorbed in God. We may liken them to gunpowder; the slightest thought of God acts like a spark and sets them at once in a blaze, whereas distracted souls are like damp wood that requires much artificial help to kindle it into a flame.

How long should mental prayer last?

No general rule can be laid down. The real answer is that if we only consider the matter in itself, the longer mental prayer can last the better for the soul; but taking into account the weakness of most souls, and the many occupations that cannot be neglected, half-an-hour in the day is a reasonable average time. If however half-an-hour appears too long, begin with fifteen minutes. One little quarter of an hour in each day is surely not too long to devote to the grandest of all occupations - conversation with God Himself. People who are constantly occupied and more devout could easily spend two half hours, one in the morning, one in the evening, in this holy exercise. The appetite for this spiritual manna will increase by satisfying it. The more you allow yourself, the more you will want. This may be said in conclusion, that the longer time you spend in fervent and humble mental prayer the more rapid will be your progress in the way of virtue.

When is the best time for mental prayer?

Most certainly early in the morning. If it be faithfully performed in the early morning, this spiritual banquet is secured, but when once the duties of the day have begun, it is far more difficult to find time. Moreover, the early morning is the quietest time, and is far less liable to interruption. The brain, being then refreshed with sleep, is more able to attend to prayer. Besides all this, God seems more inclined to give His graces to those who mortify their sloth and arise early in order to praise Him; and all those who practise mental prayer will agree that the early morning is the best time to converse with God. This seems to be the lesson conveyed by the act of the manna being rained down in the desert early in the morning and melting with the first rays of the sun, "to show that, to give you thanks, we must rise before the sun and pray to you when light begins to dawn." (*Wisdom 16, 28*).

I have no time for mental prayer

It is difficult to answer this common objection with a grave face. What it means is, "I do not want to take the trouble to make mental prayer." To say that would be at least honest. But to plead the want of time to spend 15 minutes out of the 24 hours in conversation with God is childish. What would the same persons say if they saw a way of gaining £50 or even £5 by employing one quarter of an hour in a particular pursuit well within their power? How quickly would time be found! Who is there that does not spend a quarter of an hour daily in useless conversation or idle reading or in doing nothing? I should reply, make time by arising a quarter of an hour earlier. All that is required is a little more earnestness in the one all-important business of salvation.

Where should I do mental prayer?

God is everywhere, and there is no place in which we cannot find Him, but in order to speak to Him reverently and without distraction, a private place should be sought.

"But when you pray, *go to your private room and, when you have shut your door, pray* to your Father who is in that secret place, and your Father who sees all that is done in secret will reward you." (*Matt.6. 6*).

Our Lord prescribed this secrecy to avoid ostentation and vain-glory, but another motive would be to shun distraction. But for those who have no suitable place at home, the church is always ready.

What book shall I use?[3]

For those who are able to think a little for themselves, a text of Holy Scripture is the best food for meditation, or a sentence from the *Following of Christ*. But many need their thinking to be done for them by another, and this very thing often causes a difficulty. They come across a book which furnishes them with the thoughts and reflections of a man who probably was in a completely different state, both mental and spiritual, from their own. His thoughts most excellent and fruitful for himself, are not suited to them, to their difficulties, their temptations, their duties. The consequence is that they find these thoughts "dry" - that is, they do not come home to those using the book with any force or light, although so good in themselves. As a general rule the simpler a book is the better for practical use, and each one should try to find an author, or to select some parts out of a book, suited to the needs of his own soul. If you come across one thought that strikes the mind, immediately delay upon it, as a bee on a honey flower, and strive to draw from that one thought your acts, petitions and resolutions. If the thought suggested by the book enables you thus to pray and to resolve, it has done its office; and you need by no means distress yourself even if the acts elicited and the resolution formed do not seem to have any evident and immediate connection with the previous thought.

There is one snare, as has been said above, most carefully to be avoided - that is, to stop praying in order to refer to the book for more points of reflection; for this would be to give up intercourse with God in order to entertain new thoughts. On the other hand it is well to have some other thought in store, in case you can pray no longer, and need some fresh light from the understanding to give impetus to the will. If you persist in using some book that does not suit your needs and fall in with your spiritual state, you will run the risk of suffering from a kind of mental indigestion, from trying to assimilate thoughts of another mind not fitted to be the food of your soul. The result will very probably be that you will abandon mental prayer in disgust, saying, "It's no use, I cannot meditate!" This would be as unreasonable as to give up eating because one particular kind of food disagreed with you and would not digest. Find the food that will.

Simple thoughts on the four great truths of religion, on the Passion of Our Lord, or the mystery of the Blessed Sacrament, will suit the greater number of souls; and half the difficulty vanishes when it is clearly understood that one simple thought is amply sufficient as long as it helps you to *pray*, which is the real object of the exercise. Nor is it by any means necessary always to vary the thought, for often the same reflection repeated morning after morning, will suffice to help you to pray, and if so why change it. We eat bread day after day, and if one thought nourishes the soul morning after morning why change it for another? If it begins to pall and to produce distraction, then seek for another. One holy soul found matter for prayer and union with God for months together from the two simple words " Our Father." If they were sufficient to form matter for prayer for years together, why change? Yet some people would have been inclined to pull St Francis by the habit and to say "You have been saying, 'My God and my all' for an hour now; had not you better go to the second point?"

But I become so distracted

Examine the causes of these distractions. If they arise from too great dissipation of mind during daily life, try to live more in God's presence. If from not having prepared any definite thought, to dwell upon the remedy is to have one always prepared. If from mere weakness of mind, do not be disturbed, use no violent effort but quietly turn the mind back to God. One thing at least utterly avoid, and that is to abandon mental prayer because you are distracted. By this you will please no one except the devil. He does all he can to make you give up mental prayer, because he knows full well that if you persevere in it you will be saved. If by causing you troublesome distractions he can make you abandon mental prayer, he has succeeded in his object. St Francis of Sales tells us that if in mental prayer we are able to do nothing but continually banish distractions and temptations, we shall derive great profit from the exercise and please God. What more could be desired?

Endnotes

1. *Treatise on the Love of God*. Book ii, chap. xx.
2. *Treatise on Prayer*. Part I.
3. *The Love and Passion of Our Lord Jesus Christ*, and the *Way of Salvation* both by St. Alphonsus, as also *Think Well On't* are excellent and may be had very cheaply; *Short Meditations*, by F. Luck, *Contemplations and Meditations*, translated from the French by a Sister of Mercy (five volumes, each of which may be had separately). *Meditations pour tous les jours de l'année*, by M. Hamon, Curé de S. Sulpice, are also very good but rather more advanced.

Conversational Prayer

Conversational prayer brings us closer to Jesus: it's a friendship form of prayer - it can be done while 'on the go', that is, while working, travelling, shopping, and so forth.

Throughout this booklet conversational prayer is written about as a conversation with Jesus - and also with our Father, with the Holy Spirit, with Our Lady, Saint Joseph, the other Saints and your Guardian Angel. Perhaps you too will start, if you haven't already, to engage in conversational prayer. It is not a matter of abandoning other forms of prayer, just of praying more.

ISBN: 978 1 86082 665 8

CTS Code: D 728

A world of Catholic reading at your fingertips ...

CTS

... now online
Browse 500 titles at
www.cts-online.org.uk

Catholic Faith, Life, and Truth for all